KT-451-348

Please return/renew this item by the
last date shown to avoid a charge.
Books may also be renewed by phone
and Internet. May not be renewed if
required by another reader.

www.libraries.barnet.gov.uk

BARNET
LONDON BOROUGH

First published in paperback in Great Britain in 2022 by Wayland

Copyright © Hodder and Stoughton Limited, 2019

Produced for Wayland by
White-Thomson Publishing Ltd
www.wtpub.co.uk

Editor: Sonya Newland
Design: Rocket Design (East Anglia) Ltd
Illustrations: TechType
Consultant: James Thomson

ISBN: 978 1 5263 0940 2 (hbk)
ISBN: 978 1 5263 0941 9 (pbk)

10 9 8 7 6 5 4 3 2 1

Wayland
An imprint of
Hachette Children's Group
Part of Hodder & Stoughton
Carmelite House
50 Victoria Embankment
London EC4Y 0DZ

An Hachette UK Company
www.hachette.co.uk
www.hachettechildrens.co.uk

Printed in Dubai

Picture acknowledgements:
Alamy: Minden Pictures 19b; iStock: Mantonature 4cl, Claudia Prommegger 4br, misayo 5br, juefraphoto 11b, Figure8Photos 12t, Dug Foto 12b, ivkuzmin 15m, carole.nola 16t, JBLumix 20m, LPETTET 24t, skilpad 26mr, UnicusX 26bl, hardeko 28t; Shutterstock: Mark Medcalf cover tl, Neil Roy Johnson cover tr, TippaPat cover bl, Richard Gujit Photography cover br, Photo Fun 4tl, Anna Zheludkova 4tm, quietbits 4tr, rck_953 4cr, evronphoto 4bl, Damsea 5tl, Vladislav Havrilov 5tr, Paul Reeves Photography 5bl, Kjersti Joergensen 5bm, Abeselom Zerit 6t, davemhuntphotography 6bl, davdeka 6br, cvrestan 7tl, Aleksey Stemmer 7tr, Popatov Alexander 7b, Fafarumba 8t, hsagencia 10tl, anat chant 10tr, irin-k 10ml, 14tl, 14tm, 14mc, 15t, Aleksandar Grozdanovski 10mr, pzAxe 10bl, Proshkin Aleksand 10br, Patilia 10b, frank60 11tl, Rocket Photos - HQ Stock 11tr, bffphotography 12bl, Luxana 12br, This Is Me 13t, lineartestpilot 13b, Iurii Kachkovskyi 14tr, jbmake 14ml, r.classen 14mr, Evgeniy Ayupov 14bl, Sanit Fuangnakhon 14br, Dionisvera 14bcr, snapgalleria 15b, Rudmer Zwerver 18bl, Kirsanov Valeriy Vladimirovich 18r(1), Eric Isselee 18r(2), 18r(3), 18r(5), 22tl, 23tr, photolinc 18r(4), Independent birds 19t, slhy 19tm, Heroc 20t, OljaS 20b, Andreas Haller 21t, Vitalii Hulai 22tr, 22mr, bogdan ionescu 22ml, Ulmus Media 22b, QiuJu Song 23tl, Dreamcreation 23b, vladsilver 26t, Xtremest 26ml, chattanongzen 26br, Steve Byland 27t, Erni 27b, ESB Professional 28m, Vitaly Ilyasov 28b, skapuka 29.

All design elements from Shutterstock.

Contents

Animals everywhere

Every time you step outside,
you are surrounded by wildlife.

Wildlife all around

Animals are all around you. You might not notice them at first. However, if you stop, look and listen carefully, you're sure to see or hear them. They might be ...

... burrowing in the soil

... hiding in the cracks between rocks

... sitting on the branch of a tree

... crawling up the stem of a plant

... flying in the air

... swimming in a lake

... sleeping in a pile of leaves.

Animal habitats

A habitat is anywhere that an animal lives. It could be as big as an ocean or as small as a leaf. Small habitats are called micro-habitats.

Most creatures are well adapted to their habitat. It provides everything they need to survive and raise their young. There is enough space, shelter, sunlight and shade.

ocean habitat

micro-habitat

Different diets

The plants that grow in a habitat are important. So are the other animals that live there. That's because all creatures rely on other living things for food. Different animals eat different things.

SPOT IT!

How many different habitats can you spot on the journey between home and school?

Herbivores are animals that eat plants.

Carnivores are animals that eat other animals.

Omnivores are animals that eat both plants and animals.

Types of animal

There are millions of different types, or species, of animals.

The animal kingdom

All the animals in the world are divided into two main groups. Vertebrates are animals that have a backbone. Invertebrates are animals without a backbone. Within those two big groups are smaller groups, called 'classes'.

Class: Mammals

Features:

✳ have hair or fur

✳ are warm-blooded

✳ breathe air

✳ give birth to live young

✳ drink milk from their mothers as babies

Examples: tiger, horse, human, chimpanzee, dolphin, mouse

Class: Amphibians

Features:

✳ live on land and in water

✳ have moist skin

✳ have webbed feet

✳ are cold-blooded

✳ lay eggs

Examples: frog, toad, salamander, newt

Class: Reptiles

Features:

✳ have scales instead of fur

✳ have dry skin

✳ are cold-blooded

✳ breathe air

✳ usually lay eggs

Examples: crocodile, snake, lizard, turtle, tortoise

Class: Birds

Features:

* have feathers and wings (but not all birds can fly)

* are warm-blooded

* lay eggs

Examples: eagle, starling, penguin, chicken, ostrich

Class: Fish

Features:

* have scales and fins

* are cold-blooded

* breathe underwater using gills

* lay eggs

Examples: goldfish, cod, shark, clownfish, sardine

Amazing invertebrates

Around 97 per cent of animals are invertebrates. They have no skeleton, but many have a strong outer shell. Insects and spiders are both types of invertebrate, but they have some different features. An ant is an insect. Look at the picture – how many legs does it have? What about a spider?

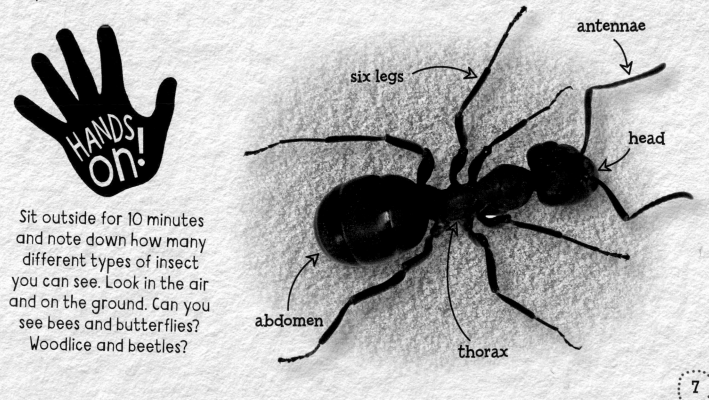

HANDS on!

Sit outside for 10 minutes and note down how many different types of insect you can see. Look in the air and on the ground. Can you see bees and butterflies? Woodlice and beetles?

antennae

six legs

head

abdomen

thorax

Make a paint trap

Can you identify animals by their footprints? Test your skills by creating this paint trap.

You will need:

* a piece of cardboard about 1 m long by 1 m wide
* a strip of white paper about 80 cm long by 30 cm wide
* wet dog food
* oil
* two strips of greaseproof paper
* poster paint
* masking tape

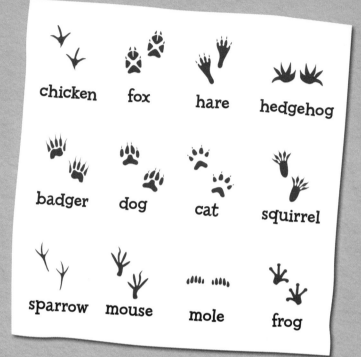

chicken · fox · hare · hedgehog

badger · dog · cat · squirrel

sparrow · mouse · mole · frog

Step 1

Fold the cardboard so that it is split into three equal sections (each section will be roughly 33 cm wide).

Step 2

Tape the strip of white paper into the centre of the middle section. There should be about 10 cm of cardboard left at each end. Put the dog food across the middle of the white paper.

Step 3

Mix the poster paint with a little oil. Spread large blobs of it on greaseproof paper. Put them on the cardboard at each end of the white paper. These are your 'ink pads'.

Step 4

Pull up the sides of the trap and attach them at the top with masking tape. Leave your trap in a clear space outside overnight. Make sure there is enough room for animals to get in and out at each end.

Step 5

The next day, check your trap! Undo the masking tape and lower the sides. Are there any footprints on the white paper? What size and shape are they? Can you guess what animal made them?

WHY NOT TRY? See if you can find any animal tracks in the wild. You might get lucky if you look in muddy areas!

Animals in the earth

The soil beneath your feet is home to hundreds of different creatures.

Earth-turners

A lot of worms means healthy soil. As worms tunnel through the ground, they break up the earth. This allows air and water in, which makes the soil rich. That's good news for plants.

Most animals that live in soil are invertebrates.

earthworm

centipede

ant

snail

woodlouse

spider

Worms do not have lungs. They breathe through their skin.

SPOT IT!

Can you spot a worm's head? It's the end nearest to the raised band on its body.

Minibeasts with lots of legs

Centipedes and millipedes like dark, damp places. They are often found in soil or rotting wood. They may seem similar, but in fact they're quite different.

Centipede

Millipede

✳ Centipedes have flat bodies.

✳ Centipedes may have between 15 and 30 pairs of legs.

✳ Centipedes have one set of legs on each body segment.

✳ Centipedes are carnivores. They eat worms, insects and spiders.

✳ Millipedes have round bodies.

✳ Millipedes may have between 20 and 50 pairs of legs.

✳ Millipedes have two sets of legs on each body segment.

✳ Millipedes are herbivores. They eat wood and dead plants.

Mole holes

Some bigger animals, such as moles, also love life underground. Moles have strong front legs with curved claws. These are perfect for digging tunnels in the earth. Moles eat worms, insects and spiders found in the soil.

Moles cannot see well, but they have a good sense of smell.

Bug hunting

Find out more about minibeasts by going on a bug hunt.

You will need:
* ✳ a magnifying glass
* ✳ a notebook and pencil

Step 1

Think about some of the places that insects and other bugs might live. Try ...

... under stones or rocks

... around flowers

... in long grass

Step 2

When you spot an insect or other bug, walk slowly and quietly towards it. Look at it closely through your magnifying glass. Try not to touch or disturb the bug. What is it doing?

Step 3

Write down what you notice about the bug. Use these questions to help you:

✳ Where is it?

✳ What colour is it?

✳ Does it have wings?

✳ How many legs does it have?

✳ What noise does it make?

✳ Is it on its own or with other bugs?

When you have finished, find another place to look.

① REMEMBER

✳ Move rocks or stones carefully. You don't want to hurt yourself or the animals that might be underneath them.

Step 4

Create a 'fact file' for each bug like the one here. Include the things you noticed about each one. Draw a picture to show what it looked like.

FACT FILE

Name: Ladybird

Found: Blade of grass

Description: Red with 9 black spots

Wings: 4

Legs: 6

Other notes:
On its own. No noise noticed.

Awesome insects

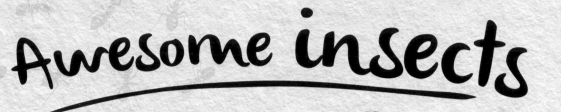

There are around a million different types of insect.

You can hardly step outside without being surrounded by insects. How many of these can you see?

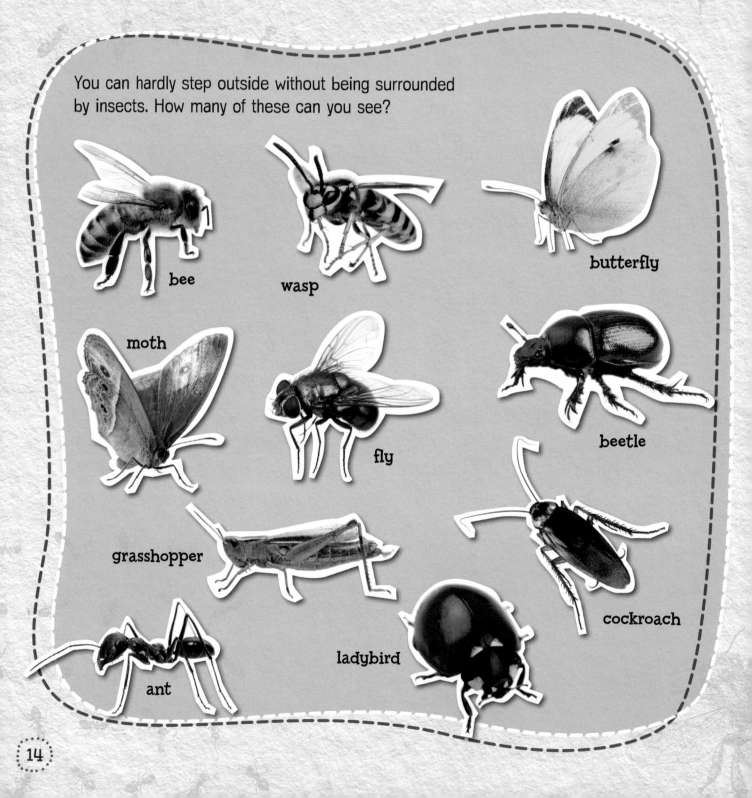

bee

wasp

butterfly

moth

fly

beetle

grasshopper

cockroach

ant

ladybird

Brilliant bees

Bees are very important to our planet. They are pollinators. This means that they carry pollen from one plant to another, which makes new plants grow. Without bees, flowers and plants would die out. Without plants, humans could not survive.

Bees also collect pollen in their pollen baskets. They take this back to their hive and use it to make honey.

Helpful ants

What happens if you're having a picnic and you drop a piece of food? You may well see a line of ants marching towards it. The ants work as a team to pick up bigger crumbs. That's because ants are social insects. They work together to build a nest, find food and raise their young. They will even band together to fight an enemy or protect themselves.

Ants can lift up to 50 times their own body weight.

The life cycle of insects

When insects hatch from eggs, they don't look anything like the adult they will become. An insect baby is called a lava. When the larva reaches a certain stage, it creates a casing round itself. This is called the pupa. Inside the pupa, the insect gradually changes. Eventually, the adult insect breaks out.

caterpillar

pupa

egg

adult butterfly

emerging butterfly

This is the life cycle of a butterfly. A caterpillar is the larva of a butterfly.

Plant a butterfly habitat

Butterflies are important pollinators. Encourage them to your local area and help keep track of butterfly populations by building a butterfly habitat.

You will need:

* three old buckets or large flower pots
* soil
* flowers from your local area
* a trowel

Step 1

Watch to see what types of butterfly come to your local area. List them in a notebook. Note down which flowers they seem to like most. Choose three or four of these flowers.

Step 2

Stand the three buckets or pots in a sunny spot outside. Put them close together so they'll make one big habitat when the plants have grown. Fill the pots with soil.

Step 3

Use the trowel to dig holes in the soil. You can plant one type of flower in each bucket, or put a mixture in each.

Step 4

Keep your flowers well watered. Check regularly to see what wildlife visits them. If you see butterfly eggs on the leaves of the plants, keep a closer eye on them. You may see an egg hatch into a caterpillar!

Step 5

Over the summer, on sunny days, spend 15 minutes watching your butterfly habitat. Keep a tally of how many of each type of butterfly visits. Do you notice any changes over the weeks?

① REMEMBER

✳ You might be able to add some of your findings to a national butterfly count. Search online for the Big Butterfly Count.

WHY NOT TRY? Attract even more butterflies to your habitat by adding a sugar-water feeder. Dissolve three teaspoons of sugar in a small bowl of bottled water. Put the bowl outside near your butterfly habitat.

Hard-to-spot animals

You might see signs of animals outside, but rarely see the animals themselves.

Creatures of the night

Nocturnal animals are animals that usually only come out at night. They might have a better chance of finding food without lots of other animals around. They may be hiding from predators during the day. Or they may be predators themselves, whose prey only comes out at night.

Special senses

To find their way around at night, nocturnal animals have super senses. They have excellent eyesight so they can see in the dark. They may have extra-good hearing too. If a small creature like a mouse can hear a predator coming, it has a chance of getting away.

Mice have big ears so they can hear well.

Here are some nocturnal animals.

bat

owl

fox

rat

mouse

Bat sounds

Bats use a special sense called echolocation. They make a high-pitched sound which bounces off objects. When the bat hears the echo of the sound, it knows how big and far away the object is.

The sound bats make is too high for humans to hear.

A winter sleep

You might only see some animals in the spring, summer and autumn. Where do they go in the winter? They are probably hibernating. That means they find a safe, warm place, and stay there for the coldest months. Animals that hibernate include bears, dormice, hedgehogs, queen bees and tortoises.

SPOT IT!

See if you can spot signs of animal life. Look for tracks, droppings and nuts that have been nibbled!

Extra fat from eating a lot in the autumn helps keep the animal alive.

The animal builds a den or nest to hibernate in.

The animal's heart rate may drop to less than 10 beats per minute.

Its breathing slows right down.

Its body temperature also drops.

Nocturnal animal spotting

Many animals like to come out at dusk. So, grab your torch and become a night-time animal detective!

You will need:
* a torch
* a notebook and pencil

TIP – Put a piece of red cellophane over the end of the torch. A red light is less likely to scare animals.

Step 1

With an adult, go outside just after the Sun has set. Let your eyes adjust to the dark, then start walking around slowly.

Step 2

As you walk, look all around you. What animals can you see? Don't just try and spot mammals. Include insects and spiders in your animal hunt. Snails and slugs love to come out at night!

* Look in flowerbeds. * Look in trees.

* Look in hedgerows. * Look in the grass.

Step 3

Don't forget to listen carefully. Sounds will tell you where you might spot animals. What can you hear?

✳ a hedgehog rustling in the undergrowth?

✳ an owl hooting in the trees?

✳ a moth fluttering around a garden light?

✳ a fox clattering near a dustbin?

✳ a nightingale singing overhead?

Step 4

When you spot an animal, write it down. Keep a tally chart to count how many you see of each species. Which nocturnal animals are most common in your garden?

Animal	Number seen
snail	卌 l
slug	卌
moth	卌 卌 ll
hedgehog	l
mouse	ll
owl	l

WHY NOT TRY?

Attract nocturnal animals to your garden by building a feeder. Make a small den out of branches. Cover the ground inside with leaves. Put a dish of water and a dish of food (such as wet dog food) in the den.

ⓘ REMEMBER

✳ Don't go out by yourself in the dark. Be extra careful when moving around – look where you are treading so you don't hurt yourself or the animals around you.

Amazing amphibians

Amphibians are not like any other vertebrates. These amazing animals spend part of their life in water and part on land.

Here are some amphibians.

frog

toad

salamander

newt

From gills to lungs

Amphibians are born in water. When they hatch, they have gills so they can breathe underwater. Later, they develop lungs so they can breathe air and live on land like mammals and reptiles.

An axolotl is a type of salamander. They are unusual because they never develop lungs. Their gills stick out from their bodies.

Frog or toad?

Are there frogs or toads in your local pond? Can you tell the difference?

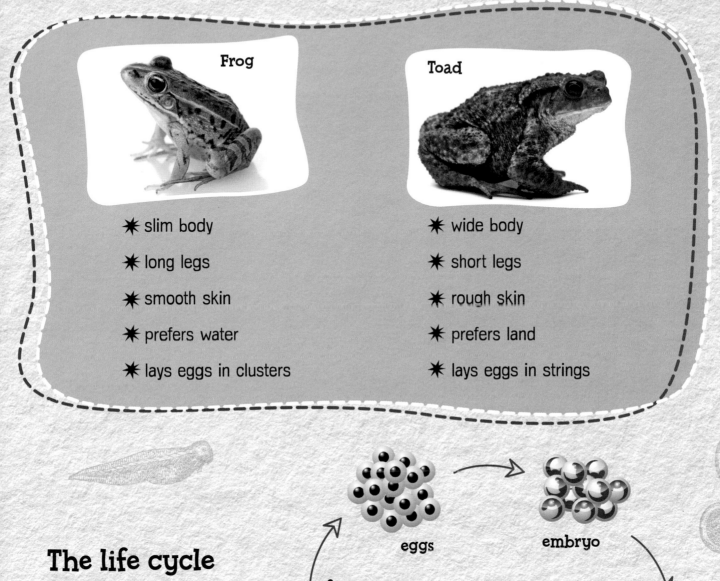

Frog

✳ slim body

✳ long legs

✳ smooth skin

✳ prefers water

✳ lays eggs in clusters

Toad

✳ wide body

✳ short legs

✳ rough skin

✳ prefers land

✳ lays eggs in strings

The life cycle of a frog

Like insects, frogs have an unusual life cycle. Baby frogs look nothing like adult frogs.

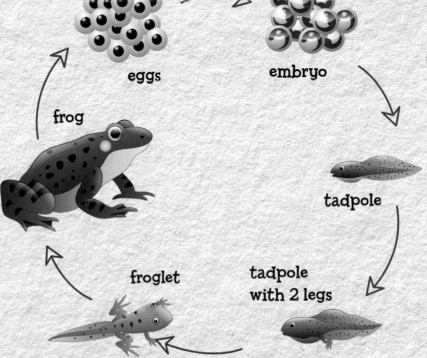

eggs

embryo

frog

tadpole

froglet

tadpole with 2 legs

Tadpole tracking

Watch a tadpole turn into a frog!

You will need:

* a net
* a jar
* a bucket or other plastic container
* a notebook and pencil

Step 1

Fill a bucket with water and leave it out in the sun for at least a day.

Step 2

With an adult present, scoop a little frogspawn from a pond using a net. Put it in a jar so you can carry it safely to your bucket.

Step 3

Put the frogspawn carefully in your bucket of sun-warmed water. Keep the bucket somewhere cool, out of direct sunlight.

Step 4

Check your bucket every three days and keep a drawing journal of the changes you see in the frogspawn. Note how long it takes for two legs to appear, then four. What other changes take place?

Step 5

When your tadpoles have turned into froglets, take them back to the pond and release them. (At this point they need land as well as water.)

SPOT IT!

Look carefully at the frogspawn. That little black dot in the middle is the tadpole.

In the air

Look up. How many different types of bird can you see?

Bird bodies

Birds are not like other creatures. They are the only animal class to have feathers and wings. They also have hollow bones, which makes them very light. It seems that birds are built to fly – but not all of them can!

Penguins can't fly, but they can swim well. Their wings are more like flippers.

Baby birds

Birds begin life as an egg. The hard shell protects the young bird inside while it is growing. When it is big and strong enough, the bird breaks the shell with its beak, then hatches.

Birds' eggs can be different sizes and colours.

sparrow

starling

blackbird

duck

Songbirds

Most birds you will hear in your garden are songbirds. Robins, wrens, goldfinches, thrushes and nightingales are all songbirds. They help to keep nature in balance by eating insects that damage plants.

Even small birds may eat up to 300 insects a day!

SPOT IT!

Next time you're out, look up into the trees. Can you spot a bird's nest?

Birds of prey

Birds of prey are hunters. They have sharp claws and sharp eyes. They can spot their prey on the ground from a long way up. When they have it in sight, they swoop down to catch it. Some birds of prey eat mice, voles and other small creatures. Others feed on fish.

Birds of prey have sharp claws to catch small animals, and hooked beaks to eat them.

Name that song

Every species of bird has a different song or call. Can you identify birds by the sounds they make?

You will need:
* ✴ binoculars
* ✴ a notebook and pencil

Step 1

Find a quiet place to sit outside. Listen carefully. You will probably hear lots of different bird calls. Focus on one of them. Choose one that sounds nearby to begin with.

Step 2

Try to 'follow' the sound. Where is it coming from? Is it moving around or coming from one place? Use your binoculars to spot the bird making the sound.

Step 3

Write down the type of bird it is. If you don't know, make a note of its size and colour so you can look it up later. Next to the bird type, describe the sound. Is it more like:

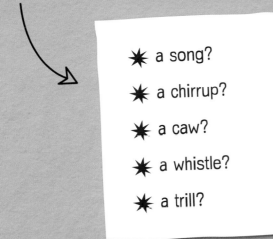

* a song?
* a chirrup?
* a caw?
* a whistle?
* a trill?

Step 4

When you have finished with the first bird, listen again. Choose a different noise and repeat Steps 2 and 3. Make notes on at least five different birds.

Step 5

Bird calls can mean different things. They might be:

* a contact call to talk to other birds
* an alarm call to warn that there's danger nearby

  a flight call made when birds are in a flock
* a 'feed me' call made by baby birds

Can you tell the difference between different sounds from the same bird species?

WHY NOT TRY?

Attract birds to your garden by making a bird feeder. Scoop out half an orange and fill it with seeds. Hang it near your window so you can see what birds come to it.

SPOT IT!

Can you hear birds 'talking'? This is when one bird calls and another answers.

Glossary

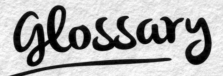

abdomen – the back part of an insect's body

adapted – changed in order to survive better in a particular environment

bug – any small insect

cold-blooded – describes animals whose body temperature changes depending on their environment

dusk – the time after the sun sets when it is nearly dark

echolocation – a special sense used by bats to find their way in the dark

gills – slits on the side of the body that allow animals to breathe underwater

habitat – the place where an animal lives

insect – a small animal that has six legs and usually wings

minibeast – a small invertebrate animal, such as a spider or an insect

nocturnal – active at night

pollen – the dusty substance inside flowers that helps make new plants

pollinator – an insect that helps plants pollinate

predator – an animal that hunts other animals for food

prey – an animal that is hunted for food by another animal

social insects – insects that live and work together in communities

species – a particular type of an animal

thorax – the middle part of an insect's body

warm-blooded – describes animals that can maintain their own body temperature

Further reading

Books

In the Animal Kingdom series
by Sarah Ridley (Wayland, 2019)

Habitats (Outdoor Science)
by Sonya Newland (Wayland, 2018)

Animals (The Curiosity Box)
by Peter Riley and Krina Patel (Franklin Watts, 2016)

Secrets of Animal Life Cycles (Science Secrets)
by Andrew Solway (Franklin Watts, 2014)

Websites

Find out more about butterflies and help identify and track them with the Big Butterfly Count.
www.bigbutterflycount.org

Explore the natural world using the BBC's earth webpages.
www.bbcearth.com/bbc-earth-kids

Discover more about all types of animals on the Animal Corner website.
https://animalcorner.co.uk

Index